Greyhound Adventures

Adventures

Terric A. Durden

Greyhound Adventures
Terric A. Durden

C.J. Durden Press
Altamonte Springs

Fascinated with the transportation industry since childhood, Terric A. Durden always had a love for travel. He found sightseeing and changes of scenery and climate not only educational but also exciting. His interactions with diverse people, exposure to various cultures, and discovery of historical sites sparked Terric's interest in travel. He was persistent about landing a position with Greyhound, where he formed lifelong friendships with drivers, supervisors, and crew members. This is a story about travel appreciation that encourages the acceptance of diverse cultures and adaptation to environmental changes. Caution: you will devolve into uproarious laughter.

Acknowledgments

I give honor and thanks to God.

Special thanks to my lovely wife, Candace, for her support with this publication. To my entire family, I thank you for your unwavering love and care.

I dedicate this book to my coworkers at Greyhound, where I have been employed for more than two decades. I've had the privilege of working with former Greyhound colleagues who have moved on to other ventures and those who have passed on, and I cherish the precious memories of our cookouts, social outings, and retired drivers' gatherings.

To the passengers I have served throughout the years, I thank you for your kind gestures, words of encouragement, employee recognition, and professional recommendations.

Contents

INTRODUCTION

I, Terric Durden, started working with Greyhound Lines on November 22, 2002, a week before the Thanksgiving rush, not knowing that I would be there for almost 21 years. Throughout this time, I've worked at the same location, the Orlando bus terminal, which is the main hub in the state of Florida. Most schedules come through the Orlando station, as it is a major transfer point for bus connections.

My first week consisted of training and getting acclimated to the bus systems. I quickly learned how to clean, fuel, remove garbage, and dispose of sewage and waste from the coach buses.

I developed the skills needed to load and unload baggage and freight from the buses. The freight was either transferred to another bus or remained inside the Orlando warehouse station. Deciphering which luggage should stay and which should be removed by hand was challenging because some luggage tags were handwritten and had no itineraries, while others had itineraries with information about transfer points and destinations. Once luggage was removed from under the bus bins, passengers claimed it outside the bus.

I was trained on how to properly move and park the coach buses on the Greyhound property in Orlando. As time passed, I grew accustomed to the bus operations. I was also cross-trained in bus ticket sales on the Trips System, which outlined destinations, dates, times, and fares. I learned the bus schedules and became familiar with the abbreviations; the directions to the north, south, east, and west regions; and the geography of all 50 US states.

I was eventually promoted from baggage agent to lead platform agent. I accepted the greater responsibility of being the lead for the overnight shift. This involved communicating with staff about the delegation of duties, scheduling drivers, and resolving customer issues to ensure the smooth operation of the terminal.

The years have flown by, and some of the coworkers, supervisors, and managers I've trained with are no longer at the company. New faces have come and gone.

Although there were several routes that I never took, I was introduced to many places. I took rides to see what certain routes were like, and I discovered relaxation and enjoyed the scenery along the way. During my leisure time, I traveled with many drivers through various states and towns, making lifelong friends along the way.

One of my most enjoyable journeys was from Baton Rouge to Shreveport, Louisiana. I will never forget that trip. In the earlier years of my Greyhound career, this was a vacation trip and a new adventure. I explored the towns along that bus route. On the two-lane highway, I saw many trees and small commercial buildings in nice, serene, and clean rural towns. I met friendly folks, felt welcomed, and was overcome with enthusiasm for scenic routes. I visited other Greyhound stations and learned how they operated. Some stations were spacious and quiet, and others were noisy and crowded.

The schedule was at least eight hours, and I passed through several communities with few options for purchasing food. After a long ride in about 75-degree weather on a hot afternoon, I remembered the hunger I felt in the bottom of my belly. On that bus route was an old, friendly Caucasian man who was selling sandwiches and sodas for a church fundraiser. I'd never seen anyone selling sandwiches on a bus! It was new to me, but I was all in for a sandwich. I said no more and happily bought and consumed what was offered. This experience was memorable because someone randomly offered me a meal to quell the hunger I felt on a long trip with few food options.

The people at each store and rest stop frequently acknowledged others with a smile. As I traveled through the small towns of Louisiana, the homes, buildings, casinos, and restaurants all reflected southern country living.

I've come across diverse cultures over the years and have gotten along with people from all over the world. It's exciting to interact with folks of different nationalities.

One evening at the station, a Polish couple got on the bus headed southbound to Miami. I asked, "Where are you from? Warsaw, Poland?"

The tall, slender, gray-haired man asked, "How do you know about our country?"

I said, "I studied geography."

The man replied, "Oh! That's how you know about our country."

I love the people from the Dominican Republic because I always ask them if they're related to Sammy Sosa or Big Papi, and that makes them laugh. The people from France are very friendly, and I ask them if they know Lance Armstrong.

Every night at work, I see Jamaican folks. When I imitate their accent, they ask me if I'm Jamaican. I tell them, "No, mon! Me not a Jamaican." And they just laugh.

Despite the problems I've had to resolve when it comes to bus schedules and missing luggage, as well as the heap of swearing I've endured, I've maintained a sense of humor, and it has been a joy to assist passengers. Come rain or shine, I've always looked forward to serving passengers and helping them get to their travel destinations.

I now invite you to enjoy my most memorable stories at "the Hound"!

"If you ever want to know about Greyhound schedules in Orlando, call Brother Terric."

-Operator, Douglas Couch (1943—2023)

CHAPTER ONE

Customer Service Delivered

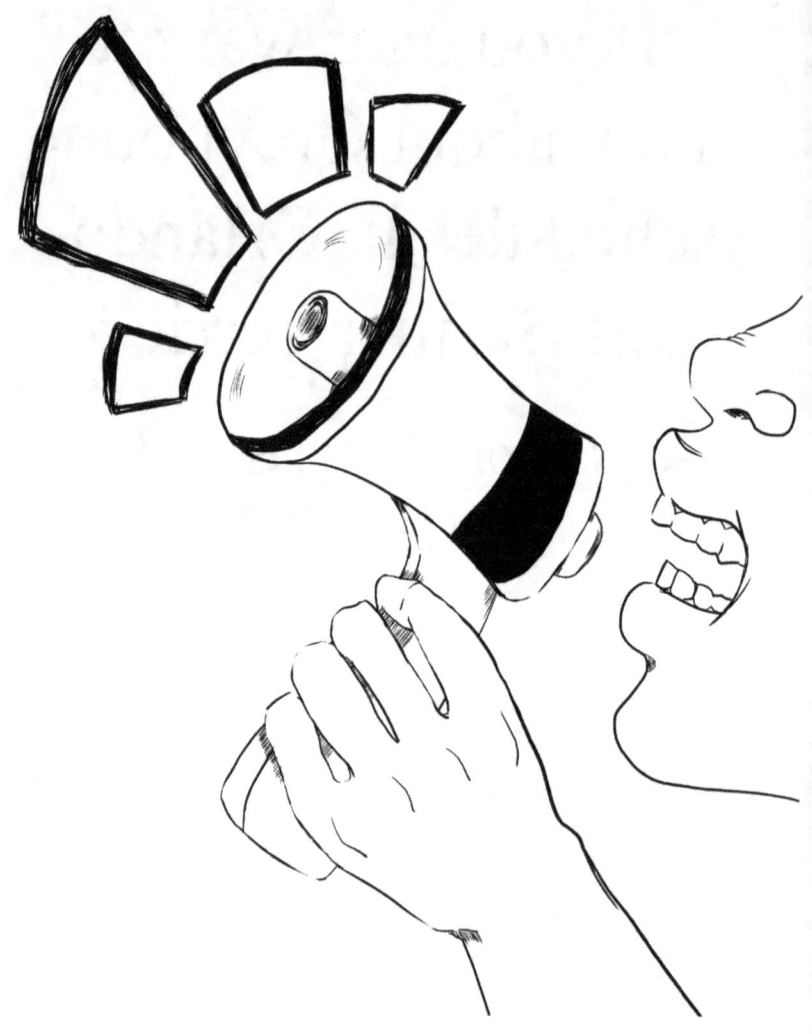

Angry Mob

As I entered the doors of the terminal at the start of my shift, the folks who'd gathered around the ticket counter raced toward me with questions.

I calmly introduced myself and my title, and then I listened to the passengers' concerns about a late bus schedule for a trip from Orlando to Panama City.

I politely responded, "Allow me to hear one person at a time." I quickly learned that their original bus departure time had passed. I instructed the passengers to have a seat and informed them that an announcement would be made once updates were relayed. I then called Central Dispatch to gather information about the bus delay.

I learned that among the passengers were four Jamaican male hotel laborers who would be working on a project at the Panama City resorts. The schedule had a delay of over six hours. I'd walked right into the problem blindsided. It was after midnight, and the scheduled departure time had passed.

I checked the passengers' tickets, including the resort workers', and issued rerouted schedules. The resort workers' originating tickets had them scheduled to connect from Orlando to Atlanta to Panama City. The rerouted schedules I issued allowed them to travel from Orlando to Panama City without the additional stop in Atlanta, and the other passengers could continue to their intended destinations.

The pressure from the people lifted, and a plan was implemented after the damage had been done. There was a sigh of relief when everyone was updated and was able to move forward with their travel plans.

The goal

• Listen to understand. There are resolutions and alternatives to explore beyond one's initial frustration.

Found Luggage

Countless bags with disconnected phone numbers are left at the Greyhound Orlando bus terminal. Some of the lost luggage has tags with names listed, but the contact numbers are no longer in service. Over the years, I've assisted customers with retrieving their lost luggage. My efforts included taking pictures of luggage, exchanging contact information with customers, and communicating with passengers about bus schedules to enable items to be transported to their intended recipients.

Here's a situation:

I noticed a black duffle bag that had an identification tag with a name but no destination. I called the number on the tag, introduced myself, and informed the passenger that his bag was still in Orlando. The traveler had made it to Fayetteville, North Carolina. I instructed the passenger that I would put his bag on a route headed to his location and that he needed to be present for its arrival. I cautioned that if he was not there for the bus's arrival, there was a possibility that his luggage would continue to ride up the road. Needless to say, the passenger was reunited with his bag.

A piece of advice

• It is recommended that passengers keep medically necessary items, such as medication, in their carry-on bags.

Straight from the Horse's Mouth

Inside the bus terminal at about 2 a.m., a slender, casually dressed White man with short blond hair, who appeared to be in his early 20s, repeatedly asked the same question: "What door do I go to get on my bus?"

I answered, "You go to Door C."

The passenger responded slowly, "Well, another passenger told me Door A."

I restated, "Please wait at Door C."

The passenger asked again, "What door do I go to get on my bus?"

I gave up. My words were clear. His words were clear. He spoke English. I spoke English. He responded when I responded; therefore, he didn't have a hearing problem. So I thought to myself, *Just go to the door that makes you happy. Go to the door that makes the most sense in your head.*

Word to the wise

• You can lead a horse to water, but you cannot make him drink.

"What time is the next bus coming?"

-Passenger

CHAPTER TWO

Stop the Bus

Late Arrival

A young Haitian lady and an older gentleman, who seemed to be her senior, walked into the bus terminal together. The older man said that he intended to drop the woman off at the station. The man showed me the ticket, and I pointed in the direction of the bus. "This is the bus right here," I said. According to the schedule, the bus was due to depart at 4:20 a.m.

I asked, "Okay, are you ready to go?"

The young woman responded, "No. We're going back to the car to get the luggage."

I went outside and informed the bus driver, "They're going back to the car to get their luggage."

With the engine running and the bus full of seated passengers, the lady bus driver said, "Okay, it's time to go. Lock me down."

I wished the driver a safe trip, and I ground-guided her to back out the bus.

The pair returned and began looking for the bus outside. The young woman asked, "What happened to the bus?"

I asked, "What time does your watch say?"

She responded, "Four twenty-five a.m."

I said, "Okay. She gone."

Point of consideration

• To avoid being left behind, be in place and on time to catch the bus. The bus is on a schedule and must proceed to its next stop.

Missed the Bus

"Where's the bus?!" a tall, slender, brown-skinned man with a low cut yelled. He'd missed the loud intercom announcement about his schedule and had consequently missed the bus too. Everyone had gotten on the bus but him.

He questioned, "What am I supposed to do now?"

Without valid justification for having missed the bus, the passenger was required to repurchase a ticket. Being spaced out without a clue is no good reason to miss the bus.

Lesson learned

• Listen and pay close attention to the announcements inside the bus terminal. The announcements are made more than once.

Left

A passenger exited the waiting line of the intended bus route, perhaps for a smoke or a rest break. As the bus departed the driveway, the lightweight woman ran after it, yelling, "Stop the bus!"

The unlucky woman had not returned in time to board the bus, so all the seats had been claimed. She was given the chance to retrieve her bags from the bus and was redirected to the station, where it was reiterated that the bus was gone.

Folks make attempts to run out the door and toward the bus to flag down the driver. Some even go as far as banging on the bus windows. The drivers just blow the horn and drive on when it's time to go. I guide the bus drivers out to departure.

Tip

• Remain alert and aware of your surroundings, and prioritize smoke and rest breaks to avoid missing the bus. Because once the bus moves, that's it!

"Do not block the seats with your bags."

-Operator, Johnny Norris

CHAPTER THREE

The Black Bag

The Bag Search

A bus arrived at the station, and the driver had left his bag on the front passenger's seat.

I was at the back of the bus, checking for left items, when the driver looked in my direction and quickly asked, "Terric, did you see who took my bag?!" The driver continued, "I bet you it was that passenger who sat near my bag."

The driver noticed a single black bag left below the bus bin, unclaimed. Luckily, the bag had a name tag with a phone number.

The driver called the number listed on the tag and asked, "Did you grab the wrong bag?"

He discovered that he was talking to the elderly woman who'd traveled alone and had sat in the front seat of the bus. She'd forgotten that her bag had been placed under the bus bin, and she'd mistaken the driver's bag for hers.

The confused lady replied, "I'm sorry. I thought that was my bag. Your bag looks just like mine!"

The takeaway

• Don't get your luggage mixed up with someone else's when traveling!

Bags Unloaded

"Why are you taking my bag off the bus? Put my bag back on the bus!" a short, heavyset woman with a medium-brown complexion shouted.

I explained, "Ma'am, I must get your bag out of the way to get the other bags off according to the bus schedule." I further explained that her items would be returned to the bus.

The woman responded, "I want to make sure my bag gets back on the bus. I wondered why you took my bag off the bus."

I reassured the passenger that her bag wouldn't be randomly thrown off the bus.

Central point

• Items are usually returned to the bus once the luggage-unloading process is complete. It is necessary to remove luggage from the bus bins to allow travelers to retrieve claimed items once their trips are completed or to transfer their baggage to another bus. Even if passengers don't fully understand what goes on behind the scenes, they are encouraged to accept that the people in charge know the process.

The Missing Bag

As passengers collected their luggage from the bus bins, a middle-aged Black woman paced frantically outside the bus terminal, proclaiming loudly, "You stole my bag!" Despite her petite stature, her voice projected loudly enough that it echoed throughout the terminal.

I responded, "Ma'am, I come in contact with hundreds of bags. Why would I suddenly decide to steal one?"

The passenger stood emphatically and rephrased her statement. "Y'all lost my bag."

I questioned, "Who lost your bag?"

The passenger suddenly remained silent.

I investigated further. "Did the bag have an address on it?"

The passenger responded, "No!"

I asked, "Did the bag have a contact number?"

The passenger answered, "No!"

Now, even more curious, I asked with the little hope I had left, "Did the bag even have a name tag?"

The passenger said, "No!"

By then, all hope was gone. I asked, "What color was the bag?"

The passenger yelled confidently, "Black!"

I slowly glanced around at the hundreds of claimed black bags inside the bus terminal. "Black? That helps a lot!"

Another perspective

• Somebody has to take the blame, and that day, it was me.

"The snake got out the bag!"
-Staff, Carlos

CHAPTER FOUR

Met by the Animals

Creatures Travel in Baggage Bins

Once the bin under the bus was opened to remove luggage, the light came on, revealing a gray-haired rat the size of a hand. The rat was discovered scampering at one heck of a speed—about five miles per hour!

Another time, a slow-moving yellow snake willfully introduced itself once the door of the baggage bin opened. The pet snake was returned to its owner before it was too late!

A suggestion

• Ensure that pets are safely secured and out of the way!

Service Dogs on the Attack

Two service dogs got into it. Their barks were loud and aggressive. The dogs' dispute lasted for about five minutes. Both passengers attempted to restrain each other's dogs inside the bus terminal!

An important lesson

• Be sure to be in control of your pets to avoid property damage and to prevent harm to others.

Travel Pets

Travelers tend to sneak pets on to buses: hamsters, cats, snakes, and who knows what else. Some also bring unimaginable items, such as outrageously huge stuffed animals. Big black, blue, and white stuffed teddy bears are seen being carried into the bus terminal.

The grounding principle

• When traveling with nonliving, yet unusual, valued, and cherished items, hold on to these treasures tightly to avoid them going missing and being sent to the lost-and-found stash.

"No smoking on the coaches or near the gas pump!"

-The signs outside

CHAPTER FIVE

Wild Episodes

Scream

A passenger stepped off the bus and screamed like a fool. But there was nothing scary near the bus.

The young, slim, casually dressed White male, who was in his late 20s or early 30s and stood six feet tall, walked in circles and screamed into the air near the bus-loading area. It was early morning—between 3 a.m. and 4 a.m.—and no one in the crowded bus terminal intervened. Those who were around just let him do his thing until he calmed down.

Things to consider

• Pay attention to your surroundings, because there are insane people walking among us who are capable of flipping out unexpectedly. Sometimes being observant is the only thing to do. But, when in doubt about your personal safety, seek help immediately. Be mindful of people who face mental health challenges and those who could possibly be dangerous.

Disorderly Conduct

In the wee hours of a chaotic morning, a traveler appeared to be under the influence. The slender, older, gray-haired White male screamed and hollered without a valid reason. The disturbed passenger, who had arrived from Ocala, Florida, was seen repeatedly slapping his face from left to right. The police were called to rectify the situation.

Moral of the story

• Sometimes law enforcement intervention is required.

911

One passenger provoked another. The aggressor appeared to be in his late 30s and high on drugs. The unruly passenger swung and whacked the other guy upside his head with a wet-floor sign. The older passenger, who looked to be in his 40s, figured that something was wrong with the aggressor and was reluctant to hit him back. The dude had used the wet-floor sign as a weapon all because the older guy wouldn't give him a cigarette. I called 911, and the police took the attacker down and arrested him. He didn't get a free cigarette that night, but he did get a free ride to jail.

The main takeaway

• Sharing is caring, but you do have the right to defend yourself when necessary.

Read the Sign

As the bus unloaded, a slender White man who looked to be in his late 50s stood right by the gas pump and lit up a cigarette. A younger-looking White male passenger with short blond hair also lit a cigarette to smoke near a fuel pump station.

A Black male passenger, who was a bystander, shouted, "You gon' blow us all up! There's fuel out here!"

Another Black male passenger yelled, "Read the sign! It says 'No Smoking'!"

The passenger who first lit his cigarette responded, "Oh crap! I didn't see the sign!"

I redirected the passengers to the smoking section at the side of the building.

Practice safety first

• If you ever catch fire, do not forget to stop, drop, and roll.

Common Bus Rules Ignored

Common bus rules are often broken. No alcohol consumption allowed on the bus is one such rule. A male passenger, who looked to be in his late 50s, was sitting at the back of the bus drunk, holding a bottle of vodka. He was instructed by the driver to exit the bus and sober up before getting on another bus. Fortunately, the inebriated traveler was cooperative and did not require security to escort him from the bus area.

Another rule that's broken too often is the one prohibiting cigarette smoking in undesignated areas of the bus terminal. The cigarette smell is sporadically emitted from inside the restroom.

In summary

• Follow the rules—especially the ones that enforce safety.

"Watch your step,
watch your step,
watch your step."

-Operator, Greg Wright

CHAPTER SIX

Gone for a Ride

Lost Keys

When I arrived at work, I intended to sanitize a parked bus in the service lane. I didn't have my set of work keys. I realized that I'd left them on the bus that I'd previously serviced. It had been a busy shift, and I'd left my ring of keys in the inside lock of the driver's compartment, the top area behind the driver's seat. As soon as I realized that the batch of keys was missing, I called the bus destination area to check for them. Those keys rode all the way from Orlando to Miami, Florida, before they were finally recovered.

The key lesson

• Keep your keys close!

Pit Stop

This was one of the pit stops of my life—one of many leisure trips with Greyhound. The bus was headed to Atlanta, Georgia, but broke down outside of Gainesville, Florida. It was after midnight as the driver coasted the bus to safety, and the passengers—myself included—sat parked in front of a closed gas station for nearly six hours. We were near a streetlight off Highway 441. Thankfully, there were no rowdy passengers. Perhaps their decision to sleep could be attributed to the nighttime, the quietness, and the 70-degree weather. Anyhow, let's hear it one time for the calm, cool, and collected folks who were headed to the ATL that night. We waited for the relief bus to arrive and then we were back on the road again.

Sometimes there's nothing to do but to wait! It was eight hours later when we got to Atlanta, but hey!

I reckon the inoperable bus was towed back to Orlando, Florida, to be repaired by a motivated, certified bus mechanic.

The core message

• Instead of being aggravated by events outside our personal control, sometimes, it is best to just go to sleep.

Long Bus Ride

Prior to joining the bus company, I traveled on the Greyhound with family members. I took a summertime trip from Orlando, Florida, to Syracuse, New York, with my grandmother, Annie; my grandmother's stepmother, Dennie Mae; Granny's brother, Tommie Lee; and his wife, Rose. This party of five was made up of senior citizens, minus one. We were prepped with snacks, dressed for the occasion, and had blankets to snuggle under. It was a relaxing trip. From the overnight journey to the daytime drive, the seniors were true soldiers who hung in there! We encountered no major delays or travel interruptions on the trip which took over 28 hours. The Hudson River, New York City traffic, subways, high-rise buildings, and water views on both sides of the interstate were amazing sights. When we arrived there and upon returning home safely at the end of the trip, our family members were there, waiting to pick us up from the bus stations.

Imagine

• An extended journey is far more enjoyable when there are no major interruptions with travel.

Arrived

Passengers tend to get excited when a trip has ended after a lengthy bus ride. Far too often, passengers miss a step as they exit the bus. Whether they're too tired to walk, too excited to get off, or there's some other reason, skipped steps happen.

As a prevention measure against a slip and fall, I or a driver stand beside the door as passengers exit the bus.

Caution

• To prevent a fall, watch those steps when you exit the bus.

www.ingramcontent.com/pod-product-compliance
Lightning Source LLC
Chambersburg PA
CBHW060357130626
46553CB00003B/1266